D1222204

Library Resources

What Would You Do with a
Dictionary?

Susan Kralovansky

Consulting Editor, Diane Craig, M.A./Reading Specialist

A Division of ABDO

ABDO
Publishing Company

visit us at www.abdopublishing.com

Published by ABDO Publishing Company, a division of ABDO, P.O. Box 398166, Minneapolis, Minnesota 55439. Copyright © 2013 by Abdo Consulting Group, Inc. International copyrights reserved in all countries. No part of this book may be reproduced in any form without written permission from the publisher. Super SandCastle™ is a trademark and logo of ABDO Publishing Company.

Printed in the United States of America, North Mankato, Minnesota
102012
012013

 PRINTED ON RECYCLED PAPER

Editor: Liz Salzmann
Content Developer: Nancy Tuminelly
Cover and Interior Design and Production: Kelly Doudna, Mighty Media, Inc.
Photo Credits: Shutterstock

Library of Congress Cataloging-in-Publication Data

Kralovansky, Susan.
 What would you do with a dictionary? / Susan Kralovansky.
  p. cm. -- (Library resources)
ISBN 978-1-61783-604-6
1. Encyclopedias and dictionaries--Juvenile literature. I. Title.
423--dc15

2012946825

Super SandCastle™ books are created by a team of professional educators, reading specialists, and content developers around five essential components—phonemic awareness, phonics, vocabulary, text comprehension, and fluency—to assist young readers as they develop reading skills and strategies and increase their general knowledge. All books are written, reviewed, and leveled for guided reading, early reading intervention, and Accelerated Reader® programs for use in shared, guided, and independent reading and writing activities to support a balanced approach to literacy instruction.

Contents

What would you do if you had a dictionary?

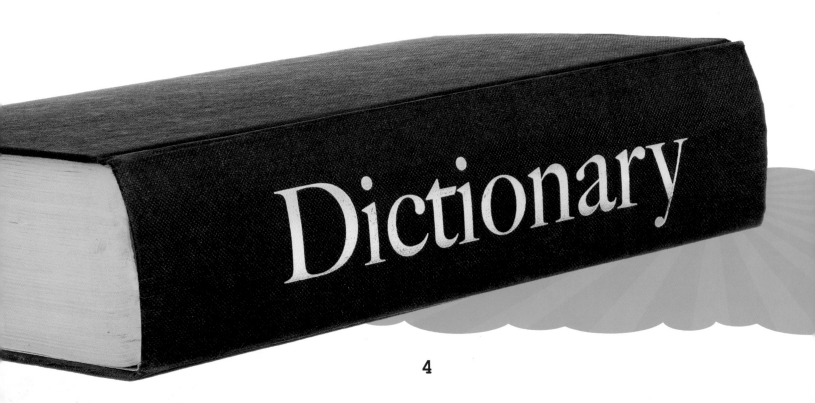

A dictionary tells you more about the words you read.

A dictionary has information about words. It shows you how to spell words. It explains what words mean.

 There are many different kinds of dictionaries. Doctors, scientists, and kids all have their own dictionaries!

Many words are words you use every day.

Some words are new ones you are just learning.

9

The word you look up is called the entry word.

A dictionary can be a book, a computer application, or a Web site.

Jack the yak yearned to yodel. He packed a sack and left his shack.

entry word

yak \\'yak\ *n* A large ox with shaggy hair. It is found in Asia, especially in Tibet. It is used as a work and food animal.

11

The entry words are in alphabetical order. The top of each page has two guide words. They are the first and last entry words on the page.

☆☆☆ Dictionaries change all the time! Old words are taken out and new words are added.

Let's say the guide words are *yacht* and *yell*. You will find the word *yak* on that page. You will not find the word *yellow*.

yacht

yell

yacht

yak

yam

yammer

yank

yap

yard

yarn

yawn

year

yearbook

yearn

yeast

yell

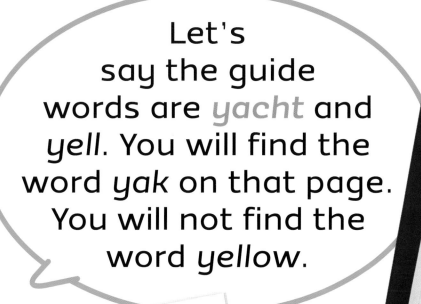

Entry words often have two or more syllables. There are dots between the syllables in these entry words.

The longest word in the *Oxford English Dictionary* is pneumonoultramicroscopicsilicovolcanoconiosis. It has nineteen syllables! It is a lung disease.

pneu·mo·no·ul·tra·mi·cro·scop·ic·sil·i·co·vol·ca·no·co·ni·o·sis

The dots separate each syllable of the word.

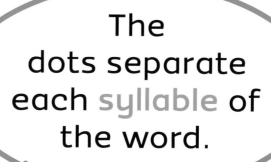

dots

wher·ev·er \hwer-'e-vər\
conj In any or all places or situations.

A second word comes right after the entry word. It might be spelled with funny-looking letters. It tells you how to say the entry word.

 Look in the front of the dictionary for a list of what sounds the funny-looking letters stand for.

The entry also tells you what part of speech the word is. It is usually written in a shortened form.

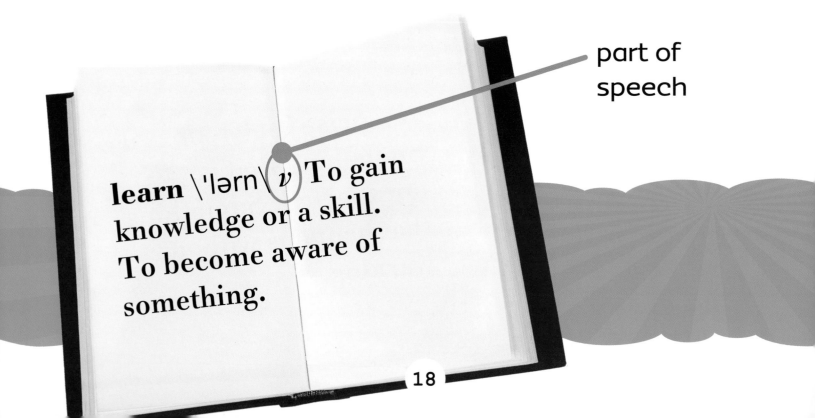

part of speech

learn \ˈlərn\ *v* To gain knowledge or a skill. To become aware of something.

Part of Speech	Short Form	What it Is	Examples
noun	*n*	a person, place, or thing	Jack, knack, prize, sack, shack, yak
verb	*v*	the act of doing something	find, go, learn, plan, yodel
adjective	*adj*	how something looks or acts	high, low, yellow
adverb	*adv*	how you do something	happily, quickly
conjunction	*conj*	a word that connects phrases	and, wherever

The main part of an entry
is the word's definition.

Jack set off
to learn the
yodeling knack.
He didn't plan
on coming back.

The definition tells you what the word means.

definition

plan \\'plan\\ *v* To intend to do something. To figure out ahead of time how you will do something.

21

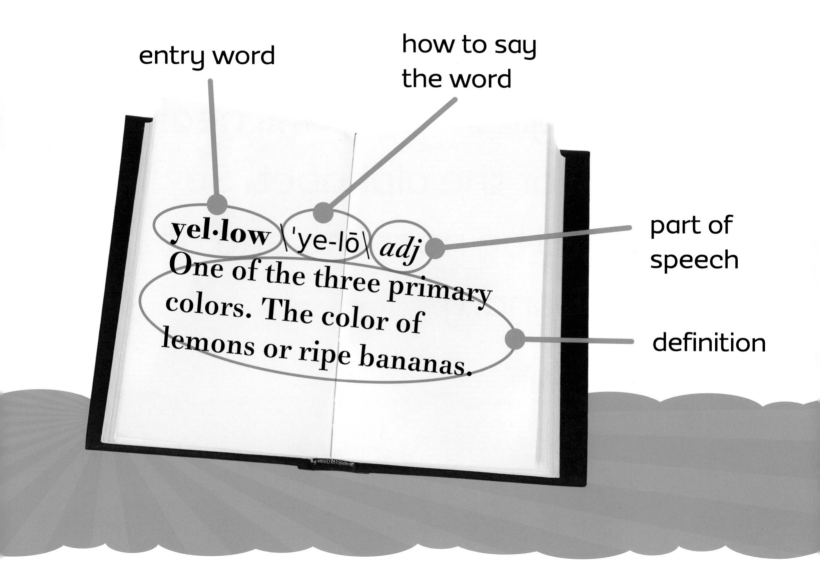

entry word

how to say the word

part of speech

definition

yel·low \\'ye-lō\\ *adj*
One of the three primary colors. The color of lemons or ripe bananas.

Yodel begins with *y*. Y is near the end of the alphabet. So *yodel* will be near the end of the dictionary.

 In English, the letter x has the fewest entry words in the dictionary.

Jack made tracks to the Alps. He quickly got some yodeling help.

Yodeling School

Is yodel a noun?

Look it up in the dictionary to find out.

25

The guide words on this page are *yellow* and *youth*.

Now read the entry words.

I found it! *Yodel* comes after *yip*, but before *yon*.

yellow　　**youth**

yellow　　yip

yen　　yodel

yes　　yon

yesterday　　you

yet　　young

yew　　your

yield　　youth

Yodeling is singing in a voice that changes between high and low sounds.

28

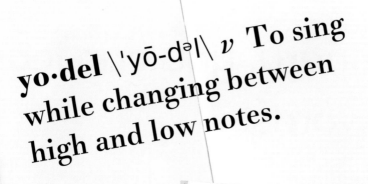

yo·del \'yō-dᵊl\ *v* To sing while changing between high and low notes.

Jack yodeled high and yodeled low. He'd happily yodel wherever he'd go.

Conclusion

With a dictionary, you can learn all kinds of words.

Jack's knack for yodeling was no surprise.
He even won a yellow prize!

Glossary

alphabetical – arranged in the order of the letters of the alphabet.

Alps – a group of high mountains in Europe.

disease – a sickness.

information – something known about an event or subject.

knack – a skill or a natural ability.

shack – a small cabin or hut.

syllable – a single sound that is a word or part of a word.

yacht – a large boat used for racing or recreation.

yearn – to want very much.